ADDICTION
OF A LOVED ONE

THERESA LILLY

ADDICTION
OF A LOVED ONE

when they say there is nothing you can do,

stop believing the lie

TATE PUBLISHING & *Enterprises*

Published by Tate Publishing & Enterprises, LLC
127 E. Trade Center Terrace | Mustang, Oklahoma 73064 USA
1.888.361.9473 | www.tatepublishing.com

Tate Publishing is committed to excellence in the publishing industry. The company reflects the philosophy established by the founders, based on Psalm 68:11,
"The Lord gave the word and great was the company of those who published it."

Book design copyright © 2010 by Tate Publishing, LLC. All rights reserved.
Cover design by Kellie Southerland
Interior design by Nathan Harmony

Published in the United States of America

ISBN: 978-1-61663-214-4
1. Self-Help: Substance Abuse & Addictions
2. Religion: Christian Life: Family
10.03.17

Dedication

This book is dedicated in loving memory of my brother David Louk, whose gifts of love and compassion will be with me always and with the multitude of those whose lives that he touched, helped, and changed forever. May his memory be blessed.

Acknowledgments

To my wonderful, devoted husband, Richard. I thank you for all of your support that you have given me over the years. It is through you that God has showed me what love truly is. Your kindness, caring, and committed devotion has helped me become who I am. I love you and have the utmost respect for you, and I am honored that you are my husband.

Dear Heavenly Father, in the glorious name of our Lord, Jesus Christ, we come to you with thanksgiving for your mercy and spiritual wisdom and understanding so we may grow in our knowledge of you. Father, may we live today for your glory, and we thank you for giving us the grace to drink the cup you have given us. Lord, we thank you for the privilege of worshiping you and receiving your wonderful promises. God, we know that Jesus Christ is your son and that he died for us, and Lord we thank you for our salvation. Today, Lord, by your grace, may we put our foolish ways aside and deposit our trust in you by releasing all that concerns us to you, the only one who will never fail us. Lord, thank you for not giving us a spirit of fear but of love, power, and sound mind, for you yourself said, "Be not afraid or dismayed," for the battle is not ours but yours, God. Today, Lord, we will rejoice in your name. Thank you for hearing our prayer. Amen.

Table of Contents

Introduction

Addiction of a Loved One has been written for anyone who may have a loved one who is afflicted and suffering with alcoholism or some other substance addiction. Author Theresa Lilly knows and understands fully just what you have been going through. In order to comfort and encourage you, she will share with you some of her deepest sorrows as well as her joyous victories, that you may also have the hope of healing to look forward to. And she is delighted to be able to tell you that truly, no matter who or how many times someone has said to you that there is nothing you can do, there is in fact something you *can* do. As you read this book, you will be gaining the knowledge you need to help you and your loved one overcome this affliction. You will be able to encourage them and support them because you will come to realize that it is possible for them to overcome this addiction.

This book is not a fictional story or a novel that was written for entertainment purposes. It is a source of informative reading material, based on the truth of God's words and his ways to receive the healing that only he can provide. You will discover how the lies and the deception that the enemy uses has been keeping your loved one in bondage.

The knowledge you gain will assist you in building the *essential foundation* that you need in order to enable you to allow the healing and restoring of you and your addicted loved ones lives. You will gain the awareness of the *assured hope of God for all of us,* that God *is more than able and more than willing* to deliver our afflicted loved ones, from the path of destruction that they are on.

You will know and understand that it is God's desire that we all prosper in all things, and that *includes* overcoming addictions. You will learn of God's way of thinking and his way of doing things and how to line up your thinking with God's thinking and how to apply his ways to your life to finally receive the peace and joy in your lives that you need. You will learn the importance and the *benefits* of forgiveness. You will learn the power of your *words* and the positive outcome that they can determine in any situation. You will gain wisdom of the power and true ability of love. You will learn how to live by faith, not misguided feelings. Even if you think you do not have the faith needed, you will discover and you will be assured that you do. You will be able to put behind you all the turmoil (commotion, havoc, confusion) of emotions that you have been living daily with for so long now. You will begin to enter into the rest of God. And you will receive comfort and understanding. And you will know that there *is* something you can do. And you will know exactly what that something is that you need to do. And you will be well able to accomplish it. Recovery is a process. Recovery is possible.

Before you begin to read the following chapters, I would like to recommend (*strongly and for your benefit*) that you please hear what this following scripture is saying. It is one of the most important ones you could benefit from at this point.

> The sower soweth the word. And these are they by the way side, where the word is sown; but when they have heard, Satan cometh im-

mediately, and taketh away the word that was
sown in their hearts.

Mark 4:14–15 (KJV)

You need to remember this scripture and the truth
of it. For how many times do we hear from someone
who has heard the Word of God and then immediately forgotten what they heard? (Why is that!) You
must sow the Word in your heart so that it cannot
be stolen from you. That is, as God has said, one of
Satan's ways to keep you from your victory.

If you do not remember God's words, then you have
not gained any of the knowledge or ability of them. Do
not let the enemy destroy the foundation of your loved
ones' recovery with this tactic. And when you read the
scriptures throughout this book, please realize that they
are not just words in a book but that these quoted scriptures are truly God's words. You are, in fact, hearing what
God himself is saying. It is just as if God himself were
sitting there and talking to you as an earthly Father. He is
giving you his perfect advice and directions for your life.
Please encourage yourself daily by taking the time to read
and study his Word and trust his Word and his ways.

Together We Will Cry, and Together We Will Heal

You Are Not Alone

I too have dealt with this destructive force for most of my life. My family and I have lost so much to this affliction. It has stolen and destroyed loved ones from my family, and it has stolen and destroyed so much of my own life. And I have seen so many others as well lose more than is bearable to watch. I truthfully and honestly can say that as hard as I tried, I could not recall a time in my life when I had ever experienced any joy or happiness. I grew up in an alcoholic family knowing only uncertainty and fear, never learning or knowing trust or the security of love. Strife was a constant and continuous condition. The shame and the guilt that I carried was so heavy during those days of my youth.

I remember never making any friends because I could never invite anyone over, for I did not want them to see what my real life was like. We never knew when we went to bed at night whether or not we would stay there till morning or have need to get up and go again, seeking refuge to either a motel or just hanging out at the airport or a restaurant *till things settled down or Dad fell asleep.* And I surely did not understand when I would see other people laughing, having fun, and speaking of good times from the past. They would even make plans for the future, looking forward to doing more and enjoying more. Oh, how I would think to myself, Is it possible that life *could* be good, fun, and enjoyable?

I would be so envious, and I would wonder why my life could not be like theirs. And I could not help but think, *What did I do so bad that I and my family deserved this life of despair?* I wanted what they had, but I never expected my life could or would ever change; it had been so long that I figured it would always be this way. And it seemed to me that it just kept getting worse instead of better. Yet, even then something very deep inside of me that I did not recognize or understand kept a small measure of hope alive. And I believe you have that small measure of hope deep inside of you as well.

You see, I know and have lived with the pain that you are living with now in your heart. I know and understand the fears that go through your mind. I know your anger and feelings of helplessness and the sickness in your stomach because my family and I have gone down the very same path of destruction that you and your family are now on. Though I lived through this affliction with my father, who finally went through AA and gained his sobriety, I never gained any true knowledge that could help when my brother was captured and destroyed by the enemy.

He struggled for several years at a young age with the same devastating affliction. Then at age twenty-five, he also was delivered and gained his sobriety. For the following twenty years, he maintained a very victorious life. He built up a very prosperous business, became a highly respected individual in the community by all, and helped lead so many to recovery. His heart was bigger than of anyone I have ever known.

Then one day the enemy decided to seek him out with a vengeance, and destroy him for all the good that he had done. The enemy took him on a four-year-long, tormenting path, continually filled with agony and confusion. My family and I and all the people who knew him could not believe what was happening right before our eyes. Those were the most devastating days of our life.

Every day I watched as my mother and father's eyes grew a little darker. Every day, I watched their heads hang a little lower and their hands twist a little tighter, the blank stares they would give each other, knowing that they each blamed themselves as well each other. After all, we all need someone to blame, right? Then they would turn and look at me with a look on their faces that broke my heart, asking, "Do you have the answers?" During those days we did not know the Lord.

Therefore, day after day, we watched, helplessly, without hope, as my brother now was being tormented, hurt, being destroyed and dying. There were many silent days, and there were many disrupted days, there were days that were filled with questions. But there were never any days that held any answers other than there's nothing you can do. It is up to them, the afflicted one, and you are to just go on with your life. And they must help themselves.

If only it were that simple. You and I know it is not that simple. In fact, we know it is impossible to just go on with your life and to not do everything that you can possibly do for them. You, your family, and your loved ones have gone through so many trials, so many difficult and defeated efforts. You have come to so many dead-end roads, and all of your efforts have just left you angry, frustrated, and exhausted with the sinking, crippling sense of helplessness watching your loved one being destroyed, maybe even dying before you. The confusion of caring, loving, and hating all entangled into a turmoil of emotions. The fear of wondering, *When, where, and how is all this going to end? Can you remember the last time you and your family had any real joy?* And with our own limited abilities and with our own limited thinking, reasoning, and understanding, we simply prepare for the worst, expect the worst, and receive the worst. But yet thank God that we *all* hold that small measure of hope within us.

You will find that you are not alone in this battle. There are an estimated eighteen million Americans that have a problem with alcoholism alone. We have widespread throughout our nation some sort of substance addiction, and it is affecting every single living person in some manner. Some are affected by the ripple effect, some by the undercurrent, but *many* are shattered, ruined, and destroyed by the tidal wave of it. But nevertheless, everyone is affected in some way or another by this destructive line of attack from our enemy of addiction. Look around at our society. Our homes and our comings and goings are no longer safe because of the crimes this affliction creates. We are not a free society anymore. We are being held in bondage to our fears and our afflictions. Our children as young as grade school age are being drawn into drugs and alcohol. Our innocent young children are even being abandoned by their own mothers, the very people who should be protecting them. So many of our children do not even know what it is to have a father. They do not know trust or security, although they will seek out these necessities. I believe it is up to us to help them find the correct way of fulfilling those needs.

Every day that we continue to close our eyes and refuse to see the truth or cover our ears and refuse to hear the truth, we lose more and more of our loved ones. And every day we are losing more and more of our young to this same path of destruction as they seek comfort, security, and love. It began as a silent war, as an unseen war. But now it is a war in which we cannot help but see and hear the screaming, shattering of destruction. Yes, we are virtually in a war. And not only do we need to do something; we need to do the right thing, and we need to do it now.

> He who observes the wind [and waits for all
> conditions to be favorable] will not sow, and
> he who regards the clouds will not reap.
> Ecclesiastes 11:4

Everything has its appointed time, and what God is saying is that *now* is the time for you to adhere to what he is telling you to do. Do not sit back and wait, hoping for your addicted loved one to do something. Do not wait to see if something changes, such as if they get a job, go into rehab, someone calls, or think that this last incident should wake them up to realize what they are doing. Do not think, *Well, today is not a good day. I need to do this or that before I can commit to helping them.* Now is the time.

The Good News

It was not until I was drawn to God by his grace and mercy that I understood. Now I can honestly say that the Lord has given me so much joy and peace, and truly in an overflowing proportion. And I know there is even more to come as I continue my walk with Jesus. And my family has healed, and God has delivered us out of all of our despair. And now (something that I did not think would ever be possible) I laugh, I have fun, I enjoy life, and I actually look forward to tomorrow and all that God has planned for my future.

I love to take my camera out and take pictures of all the beauty in this world that God has created. Sometimes the joy can actually bring me to tears because I am so grateful to God and what he has done for me and my family. And I know that it is possible for you and your family as well. Please believe me that

God can and will do it for you too. Do not say that you have tried and believed and that nothing good ever happens for you and your loved one. Do not stop here, thinking that it only happens for other people or think that those of us who say that God has changed our lives never really had it that bad or that, for some reason, we are trying to deceive you for our own gain. It is for your benefit and for God's kingdom that I share with you.

I pray of you to give your family this opportunity. Not one thing nor one person nor any situation will ever convince me that it is not possible for God to heal and restore any who ask. And that little measure of something that was within me was faith—something we all have. Yes, regardless of what you think; you will discover, you have it as well—no matter who you are or no matter where you are, no matter what you have done or not done, no matter whom your loved one is or what they have done. You and your loved one do have the faith it takes to achieve your desire to be healed and restored. And now I meditate on this scripture, and I praise the Lord for his goodness.

> [What, what would have become of me] had I
> not believed that I would see the Lord's good-
> ness in the land of the living!
>
> Psalm 27:13

I do not need to wonder what would have become of
me and my family if we had not believed in the Lord's
goodness. We know the final outcome of addiction
for the addicted and their families. If they continue
in their ways and we continue to believe that there is
nothing we can do (and I will not soften their destination for you) *they die!* It may take awhile because
the enemy likes us to suffer some before he destroys
us. There are the revolving trips to jail, to the hospital,
the rehab centers, but eventually, in the final stages of
addiction, it is the grave.

I know this to be true from the personal loss of my
brother David, when we took him, unbeknown to us,
on that final trip to the hospital. We were thinking to
ourselves "here we go again," assuming we would have
yet another chance to apply our ways to help him. But
after two days we learned his only chance of survival
was on a life support machine, and on Mothers' Day

Mom signed the papers to have him taken off of the support. Within hours our chance to help ceased.

As my family and I have said, and have heard too many times now from family members of other addicted loved ones: "If only I could have another chance I would have done more," or, "I would have tried to help them more instead of just thinking about myself." "But I was so upset with them; I was angry, confused, hurt, and crippled with helplessness. I did not see that it was their addiction and not truly them doing it on purpose." Once they are gone, we no longer have a choice to do that something more for them. What saddens me most is when they say, "I hope they know I loved them."

I pray that you make the right decision to do the right thing now. Do not be deceived into thinking, that just because your loved one may not have entered, into this visible destructive stage of this affliction yet, that their lives are not in bondage as well. Do they truly embrace life as God desires for them to, or are they content and have become complacent with just getting by each day? Have they stopped doing any of the things that they used to enjoy doing? Has their world become smaller and smaller? Do they just sit in their chairs and have their cocktails, not causing any trouble, yet not contributing or receiving or experiencing all of God's goodness that life truly does hold. Are you able to share a life with them? Do they share a life with you? Do you believe that life has more to offer, than what you and your loved one are receiving now?

It is my genuine purpose in this book, to show you the love of God and all that he can do for you and your loved one. He *can* change your situation. I ask you, what will become of you and your loved one if you give up now? But I know you have not given up, because that little measure of something inside of you (the faith) is telling you that there is hope. That faith within you is the Spirit of God. And with our own limited abilities and with our own limited thinking, reasoning, and understanding, we simply prepare for the worst, expect the worst, and receive the worst. The good news is that we are no longer limited to our own thinking, our own reasoning, our own understanding, or our own abilities. Now we can prepare for the best, expect the best, and receive the healing through the Good News!

Renew Your Thinking

God's Ability

> "For My thoughts are not your thoughts, neither are your ways My ways," says the Lord. "For as the heavens are higher than the earth, so are My ways higher than your ways and My thoughts than your thoughts."
>
> Isaiah 55:8

What is that scripture saying? It is saying that beginning now, you are going to need to accept it, that you must start thinking and doing things in a new and different way to achieve different outcomes. There are many scriptures that you can mediate on to help you in accepting God's way of thinking. Here are a few to get you started.

> Do not be conformed to this world (this age) [fashioned after and adapted to its external, superficial customs], but be transformed (changed) by the [entire] renewal of your mind [by its new ideals and its new attitude], so that you may prove [for yourselves] what is the good and acceptable and perfect will of God, *even* the thing which is good and acceptable and perfect [in His sight for you].
>
> Romans 12:2

> And be constantly renewed in the spirit of your mind [having a fresh mental and spiritual attitude].
>
> Ephesians 4:23

> Therefore we do not become discouraged (utterly spiritless, exhausted, and wearied out through fear). Though our outer man is [progressively] decaying *and* wasting away, yet our inner self is being [progressively] renewed day after day.
>
> 2 Corinthians 4:16

Renewing your mind is to stop thinking like you always have, with only the information that you have received from your friends, neighbors, television, and any other naysayers. Our thinking has been formed and shaped for many years by what we have heard and seen. If someone you know thinks one way and they tell you how they think and you have no other way to think about it, then odds are you will think that way too. How many people truly have encouraged you as opposed to the many that have discouraged you by saying there is no hope. Stop believing them and their lies. As 2 Corinthians 4:16 says, "The inward man is renewed day by day." So be patient with yourself while you learn a new way of thinking and develop a new attitude, learning his perfect will for you. You will change little by little and day by day. Do not be conformed to this world's way of thinking; be transformed to God's way of thinking. And in Deuteronomy 32:46 it says to "set your minds and hearts on all the words which I command you this day..." So make the decision *now* to set your mind to renew your thinking to line up with what God has to say about his will for you and your loved ones' lives. You will find yourself thinking from time to time with your old way of thinking (doubtful, discouraged) and that is when you will need to remember what you have read: "Be constantly renewed—having a fresh mental and spiritual attitude," (Ephesians 4:23, AMP). *Constantly* the Bible tells us, because it is a day-to-day process to a new way of thinking. Daily, give honor to God's words more than the words of others. When God says there is hope, were others say there is not, choose to believe God. A bad attitude is just a bad choice.

God tells us in Hosea 4:6 (KJV), "My people are destroyed for lack of knowledge because they have rejected knowledge..." He is saying we have rejected *his* knowledge. Let's not reject his knowledge anymore. Let's receive his knowledge and rejoice in his mercy.

> The fear of the Lord *is* the beginning of wisdom: and the knowledge of the holy *is* understanding.
> Proverbs 9:10 (KJV)

> The fear of the Lord is to hate evil: pride, and arrogance, and the evil way, and the forward mouth, do I hate.
> Proverbs 8:13 (KJV)

> Hear instruction, and be wise, and refuse it not.
> Proverbs 8:33 (KJV)

These scriptures are telling us that in order to gain the knowledge and wisdom that we need, we are to *first* fear the Lord by hating pride and arrogance (thinking we can do it our way, and take the glory when in fact, all glory be to God) and by hating the evil way (not walking in love) and the forward mouth (having a perverse mouth). Secondly, we must be wise and hear and accept his instruction and his new ideas.

> God is our Refuge and Strength [mighty *and* impenetrable to temptation], a very Present help in trouble.
>
> Psalm 46:1

We desire, we need, and we deserve all of those eighteen million lives that are being destroyed *back in our lives.* That is where they belong—with us, alongside us, and making the right decisions—and thereby receiving the good life that God intended for all. The enemy has stolen from them and us every one of their gifts and talents that God has given them to contribute to our families and our society. I know that our loved ones must have something of significance to offer us and our society, or the enemy would not try as hard as he does to deceive them and us by distracting us from the truth and lying, saying that there is nothing we can do.

And what about them, *our loved ones?* They have a God-given right as well to a life of goodness. *Look what the enemy has taken from them.* He has taken their beautiful spirit and left them "utterly spiritless"; he has taken their strength and left them "exhausted and wearied out through fear." How many times have we heard it said, "What a beautiful person when they are sober." Or that they used to be such fun and a good, kind, loving person. Well, all those good qualities are still within them. There is goodness, love, and caring, but it just needs to be restored. We are in a war, but not a war we can fight and win on our own. It is not a war we can fight with natural, ordinary weaponry such as a baseball bat or our fists, and it is not something we can pour down a toilet and flush away or crumble up and toss away. It is not something we can stomp on and crush. It is certainly not a war our afflicted ones can fight and win on their own. So then what can we use to win this war? We use God's "mighty weapons" of warfare!

> For the weapons of our warfare are not physical [weapons of flesh and blood], but they are mighty before God for the overthrow and destruction of strongholds.
>
> 2 Corinthians 10: 4

Alcoholism is described as an *uncontrollable* use of alcohol. Alcoholism is a disease. It is an addiction (dependence, need, and obsession). It is considered a stronghold that has existed since the beginning of time and will continue 'till Jesus comes back. There is no known cure yet; however, it is treatable by abstaining from it. It can be put into remission with God's mighty warfare. Many people do not understand why some people can have a few drinks and remain in control while others have a few drinks and are not able to remain in control—having one or two, then not be able to stop at that point. This is where society looks down on them (*our loved ones*), but that is due to their lack of knowledge and understanding. It is the world's way of just ignoring what is true about afflictions and strongholds.

They think that it is just a matter of willpower and that our loved ones choose this path. And they of society are deceived themselves by thinking that this problem is too big to overcome. It is too difficult to consider it other than a choice. I imagine they believe that it does not affect them. Well, addiction can and does happen to every type of person and any age. There is no one particular class of people that it chooses. Every age and walk of life is susceptible to it, just as cancer or heart attack victims or any other affliction. I believe that the majority of the addicted do have the desire to heal, whether they say it or not, but just do not believe they can—maybe because no one told them they could or truly believed enough in God's ability. Alcohol and other substances affect one's thinking and ability to make the decision to quit and to make the commitment and then take the steps of action required. You may ask, "Then how will they get that ability to quit and make the commitment and be able to take the right actions?" First of all, *they cannot do it on their own, and we cannot help them on our own. But there is one who can.*

Then he said to me, "This is what the Lord says to Zerubbabel; 'It is not by force nor by strength, but by my spirit,' says the Lord Almighty. Nothing, not even a mighty moun-

> tain, will stand in Zerubbabel's way; it will
> flatten out before him! Then Zerubbabel will
> set the final stone of the Temple in place, and
> the people will shout; "May God bless it! May
> God bless it!"
>
> Zechariah 4:6–7 (NLT)

It is not our strength. It is not our loved one's strength. It is *God's strength* that can make our mountains (our afflictions, our strongholds) flatten out before us. Our trials and tribulations, our sickness, and our enemies are also our mountains.

We need to call to remembrance that our country was founded on the principles of Christianity, but we have forsaken and abandoned God's way. It is only with God's spirit of power that we can receive healing. When we put God back to first place in our hearts, he will bless us again because he is merciful.

> Blessed (happy, fortunate, to be envied) is the
> nation whose God is the Lord, the people He
> has chosen as His heritage.
>
> Psalm 33:12

And all this assembly shall know that the Lord saves not with sword and spear for the battle is the Lord's and He will give you into our hands.

I Samuel 17:47

We need to humble ourselves before God and gain the right warfare needed to win this war. I truly know that with God's help, there is something we can do. We need to give the enemy into God's hands.

Let us test and examine our ways, and let us return to the Lord!

Let us lift up our hearts and our hands [and with them mount up in prayer] to God in heaven: We have transgressed and rebelled and you have not pardoned.

Lamentations 3:40–42

How many years have you and your loved one been struggling? How many paths of recovery have you been on that lead to just more of the same disappointments and frustrations? How many efforts have you put forth trying to find the answers? Has tough love worked? Has anger worked? Has alienation worked?

No, because you just keep testing your ways with your knowledge and efforts, hoping one will work.

I think back now to a time of putting one of the tools of the world, "tough love," to use in an effort to help my brother. After spending several hours on the phone searching again for a facility to accommodate my brother, my husband and I drove the thirty minute trip out to my brother's house. We picked him up and brought him back to a hospital that was located five minutes from our own house. We then spent the usual three hours there getting him admitted and settled in. We returned home exhausted, yet hopeful that this time he was getting the help he needed.

Shortly thereafter the sound of the phone ringing disrupted our hopeful thoughts once again. Knowing by instinct who was calling, I reluctantly answered and heard that desperate voice saying, "Theresa, please come get me, I can't stay here, this is not what I need, please don't hate me, don't be mad at me, I want to go home." I could *hear* his tears and *feel* his fear. However, my emotions were of such rage and despair by now, and that is when I decided to apply my "tool" of tough love. Even though I knew he had discharged himself and had no wallet, no money, no cell phone, was far from home, and afraid, I told him to get home the best way he could.

I then called his counselor just to have him assure me that I was using the right tool in this battle. But I assure you that neither my brother nor my family gained any healing with that action. I know now that love cannot be altered from its true meaning simply by attaching another word to it. Love's purpose is to comfort unconditionally, which you will discover in a chapter to follow. My brother made it home that night, but with a little more sorrow, despair, and self-worthlessness than he had before I put my hope in tough love and alienated him.

What have you been putting your hope in? Who have you been putting your hope in? When you put your hope in your own abilities or the abilities of others, you usually find that each effort just leaves you more hope-less and you tend to put off your hope. To rebel against God is to reject his knowledge and to do things your own way. This is just pride and our hope is deferred.

> Hope deferred makes the heart sick, but when the desire is fulfilled, it is a tree of life.
> Proverbs 13:12

But if you put your hope in God, humble yourself to God, you will not be disappointed. You have tried your way; now let's try God's ways and receive our desires.

> I am the vine, ye are the branches. He that abideth in me, and I in him, the same bring forth much fruit, for without me ye can do nothing.
>
> John 15:5 (KJV)

When you humble yourself to God and abideth in him, he will abideth in you. (To abide in him is to stay with him and his ways.) And he will stay with you and help you.

> Therefore humble yourselves [demote, lower yourselves in your own estimation] under the mighty hand of God, that in due time he may exalt you. Casting the whole of your care [all your anxieties, all your worries, all your concerns, once and for all on Him, for He cares for you watchfully].
>
> 1 Peter 5:6–7

When you apply God's words and his ways to your life, you will produce good fruits. And you learn his ways through his words. Without him, we can do nothing. With his Spirit, nothing shall be impossible. Then shall you begin to see his infinite power released into your life. I am asking you to open your heart and allow God's words to enter, humbling yourself and casting all your cares on him.

Until now, have you or your loved one been able to receive or accomplish any real healing up to now? We all know someone, directly or indirectly, who is hurting from an affliction, so if you will take a step of faith, put all your hope in God, and continue reading this book, open your heart and mind to what God is saying to you through it, and do not refuse his instructions, then you and your loved one will be on the right path to recovery.

> For You deliver an afflicted *and* humble people
> but will bring down those with haughty looks.
> For you cause my lamp to be lighted *and* to
> shine; the Lord my God illumines my darkness.
> Psalm 18:27–28

When we humble ourselves and stop rebelling against his ways, by trusting him, being patient, forgiving, being slow to anger, and honoring his word, then God will bring us out of the darkness we are in. And he will bring down those who are with the haughty looks (those who think more highly of themselves).

> For skillful and Godly wisdom shall enter into your heart, and knowledge shall be pleasant to you.
>
> Proverb 2:10

Just *knowing now that there is something you can do* is already pleasant knowledge. And I hope by now, that you *do* know that. When you gain true knowledge and understanding of God's will and correctly apply it to your life, you will know just how and what to do in every situation.

Here I will use an example of an angry situation that I found myself faced with. Anger itself is not a sin, for God says in Ephesians 4:26 , "When angry, do not sin...." so we know that it is God's will that we separate ourselves from sin. So how did I deal with this anger and yet stay in line with God's will. I knew that if I based my decision to handle it by my emotions—with my old way of thinking and my old way of doing things—the outcome would have resulted in more anger, a possible severance of some relationships that I cherished, and the person whom I was angry with would have continued to anger me.

Strife is not God's will, so I knew that was not a good option. As a result of my renewed thinking and understanding, I applied God's way to handle the situation. I first gave my anger to God. I then asked God to give me understanding and compassion for this person. I forgave the offenses, and then spoke of *only* the good qualities of this person. And God's will for all of us has manifested in harmony, peace, and a growing respect of each other. I knew what to do; I knew how to do it. I just had to choose to do! Wisdom is *knowledge guided by understanding* (having the knowledge, understanding the knowledge, and knowing how to use the knowledge correctly). When we do not understand something, we cannot make right choices; but when we have knowledgeable understanding of something, we can make wise choices and decisions that lead to good, positive, and joyful results.

God knows that sometimes it takes us a very long time of trying things our own way first and with our own thinking and planning. He knows that we will continue to struggle until we feel that we have done all *we* can possibly do (and he patiently waits for us). And then, when we have considered our ways and admit defeat, we turn to God and ask him yet again. But this time we humble ourselves and admit to him that we need him, and we can do nothing without him. God wants for us to believe and trust him. And I think you are ready to do that now, but you need to know what to believe and how to believe. That is why you must learn his words, his ways, and the truth and the trustworthiness of them.

> Sanctify them through thy truth: thy word is truth.
>
> John 17:17 (KJV)

> Many are saying of me, there is no help for him in God. Selah [pause and calmly think of that]! But you O' Lord are a shield for me, my glory and the lifter of my head. With my voice I cried to the Lord. He hears and answers me out of his holly hill. Selah [pause and calmly think of that]!
>
> Psalm 3:2–4

Think about how many people have said to you that there is no help or hope? God knew that many would say there is no help and that if the enemy can convince enough people to say that, then people would believe it. But God says he is our shield and our lifter of our heads. He has heard our voices and our cries. He will sanctify us through his word. Sanctify, meaning saving through Gods grace. *Set apart and separated to God.*

I know that you have cried out to God many times in the midst of your pain and fear, asking God for his help and guidance. He is answering if you will hear. And I have prayed relentlessly for you and your family as well. I pray every day, seeking God's love and mercy to help all of the afflicted. I would tell God, "I do not know everyone that is hurting, but I know that you do, Lord. But I do know their struggle, and I pray you comfort them and heal them. Bless them and watch over them." And in writing this book, I am honored and privileged to be his servant. And I praise him and give him all the glory, for there are so many afflicted, and they need our prayers. We need to pray for each other. Our prayers are powerful.

And the prayer (that is) of faith will save him who is sick, and the Lord will restore him; and if he has committed sins, he will be forgiven. Confess to one another therefore your faults (your slips, your false steps, your offenses, your sins) and pray (also) for one another, that you may be healed and restored (to a spiritual tone of mind and heart). The earnest (heartfelt, continued) prayer of a righteous man makes tremendous power available (dynamic in its working).

James 5:15–16

I continue to see and watch other families and close friends who are also going down the same destructive path, and I share their pain, and I pray continually for their victory. I know that God hears our prayers, and the following is a prayer that I pray, and I hope that, even in the midst of your pain, you will join me in this prayer for others as well.

Dear Heavenly Father,

We come to you today in the name of our Lord, Jesus, and we thank you today for hearing our prayers. Lord, we thank you for your mercy and your loving kindness. Lord, we ask you to give to every mom who has a child that is afflicted encouragement, strength, and hope. Lord, we ask that you bring joy back into her heart, for only you know and understand how truly heavy her sorrow is. Only you can give her the true comfort she needs. Lord, we pray that if just for today, she can find something to smile for. And, Lord, we pray for all the fathers whose child is afflicted. We know that they need your comfort, strength, and mercy as well. Lord, we pray for every brother and sister of the afflicted. We ask that you restore the bond that only brothers and sisters have. We pray also, Lord, for the children of the afflicted. Lord, give them your supernatural understanding, for they suffer so greatly. Hold them tightly in your right hand. Lord, we pray you lift them up. And we pray to you, Lord, that you will look down and see the sorrows of the spouse of the afflicted. Lord, we ask that you bless them with understanding, patience, endurance, and forgiveness. Guide them in your ways. Lord, we pray to you, and we believe that you will help us open the eyes, ears, and the minds of our afflicted ones and lead them to you.

In the name of Jesus, amen.

Some are fools (made ill) because of the way of their transgressions and are afflicted because of their iniquities. They loathe every kind of food, and they draw near to the gates of death. Then they cry to the Lord in their trouble, and He delivers them out of their distresses. He sends forth his word and heals them and rescues them from the pit and destruction.

Psalm 107:17–20

God is telling us that even though we and our afflicted loved ones have made wrong choices he is still willing, and he still desires to restore us. And he does this by sending forth his Word. Think on that. He sends forth his Word and heals them.

His Word heals them.

There is hope, and our hope is in God. Our hope is from God. Our hope is assured. Our hope has been appointed for us. It is an *oath* from God.

This was so that, by two unchangeable things [His promise and His oath] in which it is impossible for God ever to prove false *or* deceive us, we who have fled [to Him] for refuge might have mighty indwelling strength *and* strong encouragement to grasp and hold fast the hope appointed for us *and* set before [us].

Hebrews 6:18

This is God's promise to you, and his promise is unchangeable, that he has appointed hope for us. And he will give you the strength and encouragement to hold fast to it. Even if everyone else has given up, when you stand on his hope, you are not alone. God and his mighty words are standing with you.

> And it shall be that whoever shall call upon the name of the Lord (invoking, adoring, and worshipping the Lord-Christ) shall be saved.
>
> Acts 2:21

Awareness of the Enemy

God knew that many would be afflicted and need healing, and he has provided a way for us to receive healing. God understands why and what our loved ones are going through. He understands much more than we do. I'm sure that most of the time, all we see in our loved one is selfishness, self-pity, laziness, lack of willpower, and any number of other reasons that we do not understand why they do not just help themselves and change. But read here what God has to say.

All the days of the desponding and afflicted are made evil (by anxious thoughts and forebodings). But he who has a glad heart has a continual feast [regardless of circumstances].

Proverbs 15:15

"Well," you say, "where are they getting those thoughts?" It is the enemy giving them those thoughts. I know we all get those thoughts at times in our anger and frustration, yet now with our new knowledge and renewed thinking we will be able to put off those thoughts. The afflicted do not have the ability, and God knows that. Our afflicted ones are in a war with the enemy. They are filled with fearful thoughts—fearful past thoughts, fearful present thoughts, and fearful thoughts of the future. Many of their thoughts are just imaginary but can seem so real to them. The best way I can describe those thoughts would be to use the word paranoid. Anxiety is a disturbed state of mind the enemy keeps them in, giving them no rest. The enemy has a hold on them and condemns them, destroying them and those around them. They are fighting with the enemy and may not even understand that it is the enemy and believe that they have no help. At least now we know—you and I know—that it is the enemy we are fighting and that our only warfare are God's words and his ways. God's words of hope can give us a glad heart, regardless of our circumstances, because we know that our circumstances are just temporary.

> So [instead of further rebuke, now] you should rather turn and [graciously] forgive and comfort and encourage (him) to keep him from being overwhelmed by excessive sorrow and despair.
> I therefore beg you to reinstate him in your affections and assure him of your love for him.
> 2 Corinthians 2:7–8

God is (in his words, "beg of you") asking us to understand that our addicted loved ones are in bondage. We are not to alienate them but we are to reinstate them because they are sick, and the enemy continues to put evil thoughts in their heads. Thoughts such as, *You can't quit. Look how many times you have already failed. No one believes you anymore. What would you do if you quit? You will be out of your comfort zone. People will begin to expect things of you. You don't deserve a good life after all the hurt you have caused. You're not worthy.*

You need that drink or drug to get rid of your feelings and those bad thoughts you keep having. No one expects you to really quit, including yourself, so why try?

We need to encourage them to never quit quitting. Show them that we believe in them. Let them know we expect good things for them and do not expect from them anything that is beyond their means. And that we see them as God sees them, worthy. God does care about them, and he understands what they are going though, as well as us who loves them. God is asking you to graciously forgive them, comfort them, and encourage them. At this point, that may seem a little hard for some; but God will show you how to forgive, comfort, and encourage them. These are God's ways, and he will give you the ability. Jesus came because he wanted everyone to have and enjoy their life. It is God's will for everyone. It is the enemy's desire to steal our loved ones from us, and it is the enemy's desire to kill our loved ones and destroy all of our lives. And at eighteen million in the United States alone, it seems that his deception is working.

> The thief comes only in order to steal and kill and destroy, I came that they may have and

enjoy life, and have it in abundance (to the full, till it overflows).

John 10:10

Here is where you need to apply the decision you have made to commit yourself to when you cried to God for help, saying, "God, please help us. What can I do?" God is telling us he understands. He is asking us if we understand that he is telling us to live in faith, trusting him and to forgive our loved ones and all others. God is asking us to comfort and encourage each other and to love each other. In the following chapters, you will learn why and how to do all that God is asking you to do, to receive the healing you have asked him for.

We need to understand the depth of the bondage that the enemy has our loved one in and that the thief (the enemy) will continue to try and destroy them until we and our afflicted loved ones understand that God loves us so much that he sent his only begotten Son to the cross to die for us, and that with God's words we have authority and can defeat the enemy. And this you must believe: Jesus died for us and he has already overcome the world. Jesus laid down his life for us, and God warns us of the enemy.

God tells us what he will try and do and he tells us how to defeat him. God tells us that there is an enemy out there trying to destroy us and he will kill us if we (and the key here is) let him. God tells us in John 8:44 that, "For he is a liar [himself] and the father of lies *and* of all that is false." I never wanted to believe that there could really be such a thing in this world. I never believed that hell did exist. I just never believed that there was really a devil. I did not want to.

And until you accept that truth, as scary as it seems, you and your loved one will always be a targeted victim of his. It has always been said that until you first admit something and accept that there is a problem, then and only then can you change what is wrong. You can defeat the enemy, and there is only one way to do it. You have been fighting him with worldly ways and getting nowhere. It is time to learn (realize and believe) that this is a spiritual war and the only way to defeat him is with God and His words and ways. It is an absolute truth that you can receive the life God has planned for you and your loved one when you abide in Christ and realize that you have the power and the authority over the enemy. The enemy does exist, but his authority does not. Stop believing his lies.

> Be well balanced (temperate, sober of mind),
> be vigilant *and* cautious at all times; for that
> enemy of yours, the devil, roams around like a
> lion roaring [in fierce hunger], seeking some-
> one to seize upon *and* devour.
>
> 2 Peter 5:8

The enemy is seeking whom he may destroy—the whom of which are those who lack the knowledge, understanding, belief, and truth of God. Such as the case was with my family *before* we had the knowledge. Remember in Hosea 4:6 (KJV) God said, "My people are being destroyed for lack of knowledge."

Understanding Faith

Where does faith come from?

You may be thinking, *But what if I do not have faith? What if I do not consider myself a Christian? Will God hear my prayers? What if I do not think I or my loved one is worthy of God's mercy and help?* Well, you may not know it, but you do have faith, as well as your loved one. You have hope, right? Remember that small measure of something deep inside of you? And I would say the answer is yes or you would not still be reading this book. So let's hear what God has to say regarding whether you have faith or not and just where your hope has come from.

> For I say, through the grace given unto me, to every man that is among you, not to think of himself more highly than he ought to think: but to think soberly, according as God hath dealt to every man the measure of faith.
>
> Romans 12:3 (KJV)

So everyone has been given freely by God the same measure of faith. *Everyone.* He does not say *some*; he does not say just *certain ones*—but *everyone* has been given the same amount of faith, including our loved ones. And since you have hope, you have faith because faith is the essential part of hope. (Essential is the main substance of something.) God has already placed faith within your spirit. So do not let anyone else or even yourself think that you or your loved one does not have faith and the right to God's love, mercy, comfort, help, favor, healing, and all that he is. You and your loved one have all the faith you need right now. It has already been within you all along. But now you will begin to water the seed of faith that is within you, and it will grow. And every time you trust God, rely on God, and believe in God, you are watering his seed of faith, and your faith will grow.

Faith is more than believing in God. Faith *is believing* God and trusting God, acting in accordance to faith. It is not enough to say you believe; you must live accordingly, without doubt. Many believe *in* God, but faith grows as you believe God. Faith gives us peace because we believe and trust God and his promises, his promise that there is hope and that our circumstances are temporary; therefore, we are not worried and anxious all the time. And as your faith (believing God and his strength, abilities, and love) grows, so your peace grows.

> He said to them, "Because of the littleness of your faith [that is, your lack of firmly relying trust]. For truly I say to you, 'If ye have faith [that is living] like a grain of mustard seed, you can say to this mountain, "Move from here to yonder place," and it will move; and nothing shall be Impossible to you.'"
>
> Matthew 17:20

> But how are people to call upon Him Whom they have not, believed [in Whom they have no faith, on Whom they have no reliance]? And how are they to believe in Him [adhere

to, trust in, and rely upon Him] of Whom they have never heard? And how are they to hear without a preacher?

Romans 10:14

Faith comes from hearing the Word, reading the Word, and spending time in the Word. The more you spend time in the Word, the more your faith will grow. Your faith can remove the mountain of addiction. It is not impossible. It *is* possible!

So faith comes by hearing [what is told], and what is heard comes by the preaching [of the message that came from the lips] of Christ (the Messiah Himself). But I ask. Have they not heard? Indeed they have: [for the Scripture says] "Their voice [that of nature bearing God's message] has gone out to all the earth, and their words to the far bounds of the world."

Romans 10:17–18

Even if you have never heard a preacher teach or read the Bible, all you need to believe is that God is all around you. Look at the sky with all the stars, the moon, the sun, and the clouds that pour down the rain; the way the ocean stops where it is commanded to by God; the beautiful creation of all different colors displayed in our wildlife. Who could do that but God? Have you ever seen a rainbow in the sky that just takes your breath away? God created that, too, and it is speaking to us.

> I set My bow [rainbow] in the cloud, and it shall be a token *or* sign of a covenant *or* solemn pledge between Me and the earth.
>
> Genesis 9:13

So every time you see the rainbow in the sky, God is reminding us that we are in convent with him.

Examples of Faith

Here are some examples of faith from the Bible that show you how faith can heal.

From Matthew chapter 8:

When the centurion man came up to Jesus, asking him to heal his servant, and Jesus replied, "I will come." And the man said that he was not worthy (humbling himself) to have Jesus under his roof and said, "Jesus,

just speak the word, and my servant will be cured."
And Jesus said, "Truly, I have not found so much faith
as this with anyone." And from where Jesus stood,
he spoke the word, and the servant was healed. The
centurion man had faith in God's words. He believed
God's words. He asked not for himself but for another,
which is what you are doing as well. He believed that
God's words could heal. And Jesus said, "That is faith."
He humbled himself before the Lord.

From Matthew chapter 9:

When a woman had suffered for twelve years, she
said to herself, *If only I could touch his garment, I shall be
restored to health*, and Jesus said, "Take courage daugh-
ter, your faith has made you well." This woman had
suffered for twelve years, but when she spoke to herself and believed, Jesus healed her. In other words, as
you believe, Jesus will bless. And you are asking God
for yourself as well. God heals the brokenhearted and
turns our mourning into joy.

From Matthew chapter 9:

Two blind men asked Jesus to have mercy on them.
And Jesus asked of them, "Do you believe I am able
to do this?" And they replied, "Yes we believe." And
Jesus said, "According to your faith and trust and reli-

ance (on the power invested in Me) be it done to you."
And they were healed.

Did Jesus ask anything of them other than if they
believed? You may ask, "How do I believe when everything is so wrong?" Well, Jesus said in John 16:33 , "That
in the world you will have tribulation *and* trials *and* dis-
tress *and* frustration; but be of good cheer [take courage; be confident, certain, undaunted]! For I have overcome the world. [I have deprived it of power to harm
you and have conquered it for you.]" This is where the
faith in your spirit upholds you. Do you believe that if
you do not know you have something, then you cannot
use it—something as simple as finding some leftover
money in the dryer that you did not even know you had
to use? You had it, yet did not know it, so what could
it benefit you! It's the same idea (yet much more sig-
nificant) as having the knowledge that Jesus has already
overcome the world. And you can use this knowledge
now that you know you have it against the enemy and all
of your trials and tribulations—even though the truth
of it has always been there.

> He Who dwells in the secret place of the Most
> High shall remain stable and fixed under the

shadow of the Almighty [Whose power no foe can withstand].

Psalm 91:1

[Then] will he cover you with His pinions, and under His wings shall you trust and find refuge; His truth and His faithfulness are a shield and a buckler.

Psalm 91:4

A thousand may fall at your side, and ten thousand at your right hand, but it shall not come near you.

Psalm 91:7

Because you have made the Lord your refuge, and the Most High your dwelling place, there shall no evil befall you, nor any plague or calamity come near your tent.

For He will give His angels [especial] charge over you to accompany and defend and preserve you in all your ways [of obedience and service].

Psalm 91:9–11

Dwelling in the secret place is to quietly spend some time alone with God and give him thanksgiving. He is our refuge, the one we turn to and rely on. He will cover us and keep us under his wings and shield us against all evil. I know that everything around you seems wrong; but when you believe in God, he will protect you and your family. When you believe, he assigns angels to watch over you, and they will attend to your words. God's power is so infinite that no one or anything can stand against it. When you begin to walk in his way and begin to trust him and his Word and do it his way, you will see your situation changing.

The Privilege and Benefits of Faith

I believe the only thing that can limit us is our own thinking and reasoning. We need to see it to believe it. But God wants us to believe it; then we can see it. We must trust God and believe with true faith that nothing is impossible.

As I see it, it is not the *size* that we think our faith is; it is the strength (our steadfastness) of our faith that moves God. (That is a benefit we believers have.) God says to believe without doubt. And because of our faith we have patience, and we continue to believe, holding firm, during this recovery process. Do not ever doubt or give up, especially when it seems it is getting harder. That is when the real healing is about to come to pass. This is when the enemy is going to work his hardest to get you to give up, with those anxious thoughts of fear and doubt. Recognize immediately when you doubt, having a confliction with God's word, that it is the enemy.

There was a time in my life during my own recovery process that I was being tempted with everything that Satan had to use to get me to stumble. He was working overtime on my emotions. He was placing thoughts in my mind such like "You will fall eventually, so why not just get it over with now?" There was a lot of stress within our family and during this time. My brother was staying with my husband and me.

It was while my husband was working in the garage and my brother was sleeping that I felt that sickness and craving for my old way of receiving comfort. I knew that within my brother's possessions he had an old familiar friend (as we called it then) that would comfort me.

I went so far as to seek them out and I had them

in my hand and I began to tremble and cry. I fought back saying No! Satan, I have God now, and I believe you, God, and I need you. Simultaneously, I heard his gentle voice saying "I am your strength." I stopped shaking, I was not crying, I felt complete and at peace. I went directly to my husband and told him what I had just experienced, handed him the pills and walked back in the house. I lifted my hands to God with thanksgiving and praise and have not since had any craving nor desire for any of my "old friend." Every time you gain a small victory, you are weakening the enemy; and that is God working in your life.

> Now Faith is the assurance (the confirmation, the title deed) of the things [we] hope for, being the proof of things [we] do not see and the conviction of their reality [faith perceiving as real fact what is not revealed to the senses].
>
> Hebrews 11:1

So our hope is assured, and our healing that has not yet been seen (by our sense of sight) in reality is already a fact because of our faith, trust, and belief in God, that he will bring it to manifest. "We have the benefit of a title deed of hope."

A Better Way

You will need to obtain a good understanding of this chapter, A Better Way. It is here that you must take a look at what you have been striving for, as well as what efforts you have been putting forth to achieve it. I think we can agree that recovery and all that it can restore is what you are striving for. So in order to achieve this recovery, we know we must put into action some effort using our talents and beliefs. I know you are thinking, *But I have loved them, and I have been doing everything that I could do.* And I know that you have been seeking from God the ability to help your loved one. And yes, our abilities and our talents are a gift from God. But let's review some of the gifts (talents and abilities) you have sought.

Did you seek maybe more money so that you could afford another, better rehab center? Did you seek different people, maybe more educated than the others? Did you seek advice from all your friends, pastors, and doctors? Well, I am sure you did seek help everywhere you could; and it was good to seek the best medical care, the best people with the right influence—like the apostles who desired greater gifts, more talents, and more abilities. But God said that there is something that is even better to seek, and that is love.

> But earnestly desire *and* zealously cultivate the greatest *and* best gifts *and* graces (the higher gifts and the choicest graces). And yet I will show you a still more excellent way [one that is better by far and the highest of them all—love].
>
> 1 Corinthians 12:31

Love's Ability

Love, it seems, is many different things to many people, and I believe we need to gain some of God's wisdom (knowledge and understanding) concerning his way to love in order to be able to succeed in what we are striving for and succeed in what God is telling us to do in the following chapters. Understanding love is very *vital to the foundation* in the recovery process. Many think that love is a feeling; but a feeling is just that, a feeling. Yes, love can and does stir up some good feelings, but there is much more to love than just a feeling.

Love is more than an emotion, which is another word for feeling or a sensation. A feeling can create a mood or a frame of mind, and we have allowed those feeling to direct our thinking and our actions. And we do not necessarily choose our feelings, but we can choose our actions and thinking. Now love, truthful love, the love that God speaks of and teaches us is based on our faith and the love he has for us and is something that we can *choose* to do, regardless of how we are feeling. The ability to love God's way is not based on our feelings.

You need to know that it is impossible to give something that you do not have to give. If you do not have a truthful and knowledgeable understanding of God's love and *receive* it, how then could you be able to give in his way understanding and love to someone else? So you need to understand God's love for us—for you, for me, and our addicted loved ones, and even our enemies. And always keep this in mind: God does not condemn. God will with love, convict us gently, just to help guide us in the right way. He will never con-demn you, (criticize) or stop loving you. God knows everything about you. He knows everything that you have ever said or done. He knows everything that you will ever say or do. Believe it when I say that God still loves you deeply, completely, and *unconditionally*. As in Jeremiah 1:5 , "Before I formed you in the womb I knew and approved of you [as My chosen instrument], and before you were born I separated and set you apart...." Just like the majority of us who know ahead of time that the person we love will not always be perfect, yet after some time we let our feeling change our love, whereby God *does not change his love for us for any reason.*

In all of our lives there are the wants—things we desire. Yet we accept the fact and go on if all of our wants are not fulfilled. But also in all of our lives, there are the needs—things that are of necessity. We tend to misuse the word want when we should be using the word need. The word "need" has much more signifi-cance than that of want.

"Oh! I just want someone to love." or "Oh! I just want someone who loves me." We do not just want love, we need love. We do not just want to love someone, we need to love someone. Just as we need to give and receive:

appreciation; understanding; trust; consideration; security; worthiness; and a sense of being useful and helpful.

For example in this conversation one may have with a friend. "I am glad that I did call Henry to help me with this project. It fulfilled him to be helpful, appreciated, useful and worthy because of my trust in him to hold this matter private." The person allowing the other to receive is as fulfilled as the person fulfilling the others needs. Love can fulfill all these needs, yet it is not possible being we are humans to perform perfectly one hundred percent of the time. We will always at some time be disappointed in others and disappointing to others. Only God is perfect one hundred percent of the time. Only God can keep us fulfilled of our needs. We can only continuously strive for that perfection.

> And if I have prophetic powers (the gift of interpreting the divine will and purpose), and understand all the secret truths and mysteries and possess all knowledge, and if I have [sufficient] faith so that I can remove mountains, but have not love (God's love in me) I am nothing (a useless nobody).
>
> 1 Corinthians 13:2

- Love is being, respectful (reverential, reverent, polite)
- God respects you
- Love is faithful (true, constant, dedicated, devoted, committed)
- God is faithful to you
- Love is patient (long suffering, tolerant being steadfast)
- God is patient with you
- Love is Forgiveness (letting go of an offense giving it to God)
- God forgives you
- Love is putting others needs before your needs.
- God will fill all your needs.

I must admit that I did struggle with putting others' needs before my needs in certain situations such as my time. I always questioned, "When do I get to do what I feel is important to me?" It left me so frustrated, and I began to allow resentment to build up in me. Then I remembered that I must not be doing something God's way because I had no peace with this resentment. I then trusted God and said to him, "Okay, God. I will do it your way, and I will trust you to give me the time to do what I feel I need to do and get done." I gave my resentment to God, trusted him, and gave my time to others first; and before I knew it, somehow, time for me became available, and it was peaceful and productive. I stopped wanting it my way and did it God's way, and it worked.

Love is the highest and the choicest gift we should seek from God. And with love, we can choose to be patient, we can choose to be faithful, and we can choose to be forgiving, regardless of our "feelings." You also need to love yourself—not in a fleshly, selfish way, but in all the ways described above. Respect yourself, be patient with yourself, and forgive yourself. God said in Galatians 6:1 (KJV), "Considering thyself…" We are to love others as we love ourselves, so remember to love yourself as well. Sometimes, we just love someone; it is easy. It just happens; we did not have to choose to love them. We just knew we loved them. We want them safe. We want them healed. We respect them, are polite to them. And we understand them, comfort them, and encourage them. We forgive them. We are patient, faithful, kind, helpful, honest, and compassionate, and we sacrifice for them.

But then time goes on and our feelings change, and we begin to allow our hurt feelings and bitterness and anger to start motivating us. You see, we loved them based on our feelings. We forgot the reason we respected them, and we began to focus on some small offense. And rather than letting it go, we would dwell on it, and continue to add other small offenses to our feelings, therefore hardening our hearts against them and then basing our love on our feelings.

You see, love is a choice we can make. Love is an action we can take. So when they say there is nothing you can do, you know you can love them. The best way to learn and receive God's love is not by me or someone else telling you but by reading his Word and letting him plant his Word within you himself. And by loving others, you will be able to see his love for you. It is the best way to truly receive his love and understand it.

> But when the Holy Spirit controls our lives, he
> will produce this kind of fruit in us: love, joy,
> peace, patience, kindness, goodness, faithful-

ness, gentleness, and self control. Here there is
no conflict with the law.

Galatians 5:22–23 (NLT)

The Holy Spirit will give you all these gifts if you
seek them. Allow Jesus to enter into your heart and
accepting him. Trust him, giving him all your concerns, and praising him for the work he is doing in
your life. Believe he is working everything out while
you wait patiently for his favor and his mercy. You
will see God's hand working in your life when you
make the decision and begin walking in love with a
forgiving heart, with a patient spirit, and with a hopeful, expectant attitude. Remember that your attitude
affects other people. And when you have a good attitude, it can only help improve others' attitudes. That
is doing something God's way.

> For if you love those who love you, what reward
> can you have? Do not even the tax collectors do
> that? And if you greet only your brethren, what
> more than others are you doing? Do not even
> the Gentiles (the heathen) do that? You there-
> fore, must be perfect [growing into complete
> maturity of godliness in mind and character,

having reached the proper height of virtue and integrity], as your heavenly Father is perfect.

Matthew 5:46–48

So we must do different than that of the world's way, by doing more than that of what others are doing. Being in the world not of the world, not conforming to their ways.

When God asks us to love our neighbor and to love our enemy, right away, we associate that with our feelings. And we allow our feelings to motivate us, which determines our actions. Instead, we need to choose to love, therefore doing it God's way, the better way.

I had a coworker at one time that, from the first day, took a disliking to me and made no secret about it. This person was downright rude to me. So I applied God's way to the situation by praying every day for her, treating her with respect, forgiving her actions, and I was patient. The next thing I knew, this person came to me and needed a friend. I thanked God for the truth of his words and his way. I could have treated this person the way she treated me, but I chose to walk in love regardless of how I felt, and God rewarded me with a friend.

What helps me is that at the very least, I can choose to respect the life of my enemy that God has created. When I find it hard to get my flesh in agreement to pray for my enemy, I just have to remind myself that I cannot change what they have done. But would I want them to continue doing the unjust thing, or would I rather they be able to change? It does not require feelings, just a right action.

> No one has greater love [no one has shown stronger affection] than to lay down (give up) his own life for his friends.
>
> John 15:13

I believe that most people are followers so to speak and that they will eventually follow you. Be the leader God needs you to be. Lead them with love, courage, strength, understanding, hope, and comfort. *Exalt them, and God will exalt you.*

A Step of Faith
in Forgiveness

For My thoughts are not your thoughts, neither are your ways My ways, says the Lord.
For as the heavens are higher than the earth,
so are My ways higher than your ways, and
My thoughts than your thoughts.

Isaiah 55:8–9

Forgiveness is another action step that you will need
to take in order for the healing process to truly begin.
You can do this with your new assured hope, faith, and
renewed thinking and attitude. Remember when every-

one said there is nothing you can do, and you began to
believe them when everything you did do failed? Well,
let's prove them wrong starting now. The next step you
must take, now that you have chosen to love and knowing that you have the faith and the hope of winning
this battle, is forgiveness. This is God's way, remember?
With our faith (believing and trusting God), we must
walk in his way and do it his way. It is not hard, just
different. It does not hurt; it *heals*.

> And be ye kind one to another tenderhearted
> forgiving one another even as God for Christ
> sake hath forgiven you.
>
> Ephesians 4:32

This is truly one of the most important steps of faith
that you will take. And it is, I believe, the most mis-
understood act of faith that there is. I believe that it is
one of the largest stumbling blocks that we can ever
encounter. We need to see that un-forgiveness is one
of Satan's greatest weapons that he uses against us to
keep our loved one and ourselves in bondage. He has
the world so deceived of the true knowledge (true
perception of truth) and understanding (nature and

significance) of forgiveness, which deludes us of the wisdom and the ability to choose the right decision: to forgive and allow God's healing into our lives.

The devil knows that forgiveness is essential (the main substance) to healing and that un-forgiveness is a major cause of sickness. If you have knowledge and understanding of this, you will be able to overcome the obstacles that you and your loved one are going to face as you go through the healing process. I do not want you and your loved ones to get to that wonderful step in the healing process and then stumble and fail (be destroyed) because of lack of knowledge. This step of faith is not intended to show an acceptance of an offense, nor is it to express a willingness to allow further deceptions or offenses. It is not a felt emotion; it is an act of faith that you put into action. It is giving the hurt or the offense to God and then remembering it no more, letting it go and pardoning it. Un-forgiveness is *very heavy* to carry around in your heart, and when you learn to trust God and give him all of your hurt, believing that he will right all the wrongs done to you, you will be amazed at how good you will begin to feel. And we forgive for Christ's sake, just as God forgives us for Christ's sake. So then who are we not to forgive?

I remember one day driving to work, feeling so unworthy of God's love, and I asked him, "God, why do you forgive me?" and he said, "For my Son's sake and that I love you, and you have forgiven others." I knew the rest of that day that I was not worthless.

> O Lord God, You to whom vengeance be-
> longs, O God you to whom vengeance be-
> longs, Shine forth!
>
> Psalm 94:1

God gives us the ability to forgive. We have the privilege and ability *to give to God* all of the offenses directed against us, letting them go and remembering them no more, not allowing them to take root, altering our focus on love. Of course, in time the enemy is going to remind you of such offenses that you have already decided on and given to God. And when that happens, you must then immediately think and say, "No, Satan. I have gained the wisdom and knowledge on this, and I no longer own that offense. I have given it to God, who is my avenger. I no longer hold onto the heaviness of un-forgiveness in my heart." If you do not let it go and trust God to make right all the wrongs that have been done to you, you will continue to think on the offense, which will rise up the bad emotions, causing you to take the wrong actions. And it will harden your heart. And when your heart is hardened, you cannot let God's words and his ways in. Remember that forgiveness is essential (the main substance) to healing. The enemy is going to work his hardest to trip you up on this step of faith, so be aware at all times.

There must be something of significance to forgiving because God reminds us daily in the Lord's Prayer to forgive one another. This is the prayer that Jesus instructed us to pray.

> After this manner therefore pray ye: "Our Father, who art in heaven, Hallowed be thy name, thy kingdom Come, thy will be done on earth as it is in heaven. Give us this day our daily Bread and forgive us our trespasses as We forgive those who trespass against us. And lead us not into temptation, But deliver us from evil. For thine is the Kingdom, the power and the glory forever and ever."
>
> Matthew 6:9–13 (KJV)

God is leading us in this step away from sinning. When you really and truly understand how this can change situations, you will be amazed. This is God's way, and his is the way. Remember, do not listen to the enemy. You want God to hear and answer your prayers for you and your loved one. Remember. Hear his instruction, and do not refuse it.

> And whenever you stand praying, if You have anything against anyone, Forgive him *and* let it drop (leave it, Let it go), in order that your Father who is in Heaven may also forgive you your (own) failing *and* shortcomings *and* let them drop. But if you do not forgive, neither will your Father in heaven forgive your failings and shortcomings.
>
> Mark 11:25–26

Forgiving is not hard to do; it is just different than what we are used to doing. And it brings us into obedience to God. Remember our old ways, the anger, the blaming each other, the silent days holding on to the pain and hurt, and the tough love. Forgiving is truly God's way.

This does not always mean that the best thing to

do is to just walk up to them and say, "I forgive you." It is best when we do this from our hearts, by *showing* it in the way that we treat others. Our actions and words will illustrate a forgiving nature. We will not be speaking with a hidden bitterness in our tone of voice or gestures. They will feel and see your forgiveness, and the best part of this is, that they will see your understanding and loving them. When we do not forgive, we speak with a bitter voice and attitude, and our loved ones perceive it as condemnation.

I know you have experienced and still do hold many angry emotions, and not just toward your loved one but toward their friends and associates, assuming they are a main contributing factor to enticing the wrong influence, and more than likely toward someone who may be their source of acquiring their substance. Unfortunately the day of prohibition has passed, and the only way to stop the drug traffic is to stop the demand of the evil substance. I am certain you hold a notable amount of anger towards some of your immediate family as well. It always seemed to me that most of their "helpful suggestions" held no realistic understanding nor knowledge. I pray, though, that you draw on God's strength and his mercy and pray for those that you are angry with. There are many reasons to feel anger, but rely on this.

> Assuredly [I pledge it] The wicked shall not go unpunished, but the multitude of The [un-compromisingly] righteous shall be delivered.
>
> Proverbs 11:21

We must all admit that we are all sinners in order to be truthful and be able to receive God's truth.

> If we say we have no sin [refusing to admit that we are sinners]. We delude *and* lead ourselves astray, and the Truth [which the Gospel presents] is not in us [does not dwell in our hearts].
> If we [freely] admit that we have sinned *and* confess our sins. He is faithful and just (true to His own nature and promises) and will forgive our sins [dismiss our lawlessness] and [continuously] cleanse us from all unrighteousness [everything not in conformity to His will in purpose, thought, and action].
>
> I John 1:8–9

In this scripture above, please grasp the meaning of the word continuously (meaning: unbroken, uninterrupted and endless). God continuously cleanses us.

We need to receive God's forgiveness so that we ourselves posses it, allowing us to continuously pass it along to others.

> But if ye forgive not men their Trespasses, neither will, your father Forgive your trespasses.
> Matthew 6:15 (KJV)

So we must give it freely and readily. We cannot give it expecting something in return, such as, "I'll forgive you if you do this or that for me." You cannot sell it, buy it, or trade for it. We have been living in un-forgiveness for so long now that it is going to take some practice getting to the point that you can readily do this, but you will get there.

> If you forgive anyone anything, I too forgive that one; and what I have forgiven, if I have forgiven anything, has been for your sakes in the presence [and with the approval] of Christ (the Messiah).
> 2 Corinthians 2:10

This is not something you are to do only once and it is done, but this is to become a part of your daily life. Remember our daily prayers. Every day, the enemy is just waiting for an open door to sneak into. And remember that our choices and our actions do affect others. This is something that you can do. It is a spiritual weapon that you are applying to the war.

> To keep Satan from getting the advantage over us; for we are not ignorant of his wiles and intentions.
>
> 2 Corinthians 2:11

Not only do you need to apply this to past offences, but future offenses as well. One reason is because once you begin to see with your own eyes the healing process taking place and your loved ones beginning to attend meetings, meet new people, get out and become less dependent on you, you will begin to feel somewhat left behind. Where does that leave you? This is where you must be aware of the enemy once again. (He will always be waiting on the side for any opening he can find.) He will work overtime on your emotions and feelings with suggestions such as, "Ha!

Look at them now, and just look at yourself. There they are off having a good time, looking good now, and here you are sitting at home alone. And after all you have done for them." In fact, there are going to be many, many things that the enemy is going to try to get you stirred up over. So beware, and remember to speak to him with your new knowledge and wisdom.

Remember what God said. You are to reinstate them in your affections and assure them of your love. To not do this has been a leading cause of relapse. So you need to reassure them of your love by giving them the encouragement they need to continue going to meetings, not by letting their going to meetings cause strife, therefore giving the enemy no cause to give them thoughts such as, *Well, this is no better than before. I just can't please them no matter what I do.* Learn to start enjoying the time of peace you have. Continue to read this book a few times. Spend time with God. Think of the great future you now have ahead of you. When they come home after attending a meeting, be available and encouraging, willing to just listen, not asking a lot of third degree questions. And if you had problems to handle while they were at the meeting, consider them just that—handled! Do not burden them with the idea that they should have been there assisting you with something that you were able to handle.

> Brethren, if a man be overtaken in a fault, ye which are spiritual, restore such a one in the spirit of meekness; considering thyself, least thou also be tempted. Bear ye one another's burdens, and so fulfill the law of Christ.
>
> Galatians 6:1–2

Before we go any further, please read the following with a focused attention.

God never has and never will, not now or ever, expect you to be a victim of any kind whatsoever—not financially, not emotionally, not physically, not by verbal abuse, or in any manor for even one minute. God says to consider yourself. When we begin to help our loved ones, we need to know and understand the difference between what is true help and what is considered enabling them to continue on their destructive paths. You need to understand that loving someone means making the right choice and taking the right action, regardless of our emotions, fears, and doubts.

We all know it can be extremely difficult, almost to the point of impossible, to make the right choice and then to actually take the right action when it feels like it is going to break our hearts to do it—especially when we think there is a chance we will lose our connection or contact with our loved one because of it. You've heard before, "I'll never talk to you again, thanks for nothing." Knowing everything and being in the midst of it all is difficult. Not knowing is even harder. But we must not allow them to use us beyond our means. They certainly know how to work our emotions, beg for money, and verbally make a point. And because we never knew what else we could do, we contributed the only thing we had to contribute at the time. Now you will learn how to help them and know that you have made the right decision, not continuing in that roller coaster of emotions. You will be stronger and more confident for the next confrontation.

> [It is then] my counsel *and* my opinion in this matter that I give [you when I say]: It is profitable *and* fitting for you [now to complete the enterprise] which more than a year ago you not only began, but were the first to wish to do anything [about contributions for the relief of the saints at Jerusalem].
>
> So now finish doing it, that your [enthusiastic] readiness in desiring it may be equaled

by your completion of it according to your
ability *and* means.

For if the [eager] readiness to give is there,
then it is acceptable and welcomed in proportion to what a person has, not according to
what he does not have.

For it is not [intended] that other people
be eased and relieved [of their responsibility]
and you be burdened and suffer [unfairly].

II Corinthians 8:10–13

You will begin to learn to talk to God and wait on
God with patience. God will give you all the understanding you need with his words. As we have read in
the scripture above, that scripture is one that has help
me many times in knowing how much God wants me
to do. You will begin to learn to listen and act according to that small, still voice in your heart, not that
voice of the anxious, negative enemy in your head.

When you have considered all things, and believe
you have made a decision that lines up with God's
words on how to handle a situation, then bring it to
God, wait and see if you receive a peace about it. If
you truly have peace, go ahead move forward. If you
do not have the peace, then I would wait on God

to move things forward. You should find a spot by yourself and just sit quietly and fellowship with God. You have a right to set some boundaries, such as your quiet spot. No interruptions allowed. The enemy will certainly try and disturb you with things such as the phone ringing, outside distractions and such, but do not omit this practice in your prayer time.

Bearing another's burdens is just lightening their load. Being forgiving lightens their load of condemnation; it lightens their load of guilt. Gently remind them, with meekness, that they have choices. Do not be harsh or critical. The enemy translates to them that they are not loved and are not worthy of kindness if you are harsh or critical.

> But verily God, hath heard me; He hath attended to the voice of my Prayer. Blessed be God, which hath not turned away my prayer, nor his mercy from me.
>
> Psalm 66:19–20 (KJV)

Our Father in heaven does hear our prayers, and he does love us, and God does want to help us. And God will help us. And his mercy is new everyday. So everyday, no matter what we did yesterday, he still loves us today. But we need to listen to him, trust him, and abide in him. We need to humble ourselves to him. We need to *accept his words and accept his help*. And God hears our prayers for others. We can pray for God's forgiveness of others, and he will pardon them, just as we read in 2 Chronicles 30:18–20 . King Hezekiah prayed for the multitude of the people who had not complied, saying, "May the Lord pardon everyone," and the Lord harkened to King Hezekiah and healed the people. It is God's nature to forgive. And God made us in his likeness. So when we walk and live in forgiveness, it puts us into the natural state that God intended for us. Bringing us into that spirit of rest.

Consider how you feel when you are in an unnatural situation, somewhere you are not normally at, or around unfamiliar surroundings with people you are not normally around? Do you feel a little uneasy, not so at peace or comfortable, and eager to get back to where you are more naturally accustomed? That is how it is we get into our un-natural state of un-forgiveness. But when we get into God's natural state of forgiveness we receive the true spirit of peace. I know that people will say things to you such as, "How can you forgive them after all that they have done? What has come over you?" Just smile and peacefully say, "God has."

Un-forgiveness cannot change the past, but it can destroy a future. Forgiveness cannot change the past, but it can *restore a future*. Forgiveness honors Christ. It shows him that you are humbling yourself before God and accepting his way, believing him and trusting him. And it removes the mountain of guilt from your loved one.

> He leads the humble in what is right,
>> And the humble He teaches His way.
>>>> Psalm 25:9

The Power of Faith-filled Words

In this chapter, you will learn just how *powerful* the words you choose to speak are and how you can choose the right words to speak. The words you *speak* can determine the final outcome of any situation. There are well over five hundred verses in the Bible that teach us how to choose our words and why to choose the right words. Words provide, make available the *power* that we hold with our tongue. It is *very important* that you gain the understanding of *your authority* in Jesus with God's words. They are mighty. They are your *weapon against this addiction* of your loved one. They can release the strongholds, flatten the mountains, and provide the healing.

> And [the angle] said to me, "O Daniel, you greatly beloved man, understand the words that I speak to you and stand upright, for to you I am now sent." And while he was saying this word to me, I stood up trembling. Then he said to me. "Fear not, Daniel, for from the first day that you set your mind *and* heart to understand and to humble yourself before your God, your words were heard, and I have come as a consequence of [and in response to] your words."
>
> Daniel 10:11–12

God has heard your prayers.

I pray that you are trembling just as Daniel trembled, as *you personally* receive this scripture in your heart.

Your words were heard by God, your cries and your prayers and supplications. And he has sent an angel in response to "Your" words in prayer.

Death and Life are in the Power Of the tongue
and they who indulge in it shall eat the fruit of
it [for death or life].

Proverb 18:21

Please think on that scripture. Meditate and pray on
what God is saying in that verse. God is telling us that
death and life are in the *power of the tongue*, therefore showing *the power* of the words we speak. *Power*
means authority, control, directive, influence, command over, to rule, and to manage. With our words,
we have *authority* over the enemy. We can direct the
way situations go. You must have faith and believe
(trusting God and his ability). God works through
our speaking the word boldly with confidence and
with our assured hope. And we have the ability to
influence others with our words. God said that he has
set before us life and death. Choose life. Abiding in
his words and ways are life. And he says that we will
eat the fruit of it. The words you speak and sow are
going to produce what you receive (harvest).

God's Word is truth (fact, reality, certainty). God's
Word is reliable (dependable, unfailing, consistent).
God's Word is trustworthy (honest, honorable). God's

Word is consistent (steady, constant). Therefore, your words also need to be truthful, reliable, trustworthy, and consistent. Remember, Psalm 107:20 says, "God sends forth his word and heals them and rescues them from the pit of destruction." God is sending forth his word, and he needs you and me to speak them. When we read and study the Bible, we see how God brought everything to manifest (make visible, to make observable) with his words.

> And God *said*,
>> "Let there be light…"
>
> And God *said*,
>> "Let there be a firmament…"
>
> And God *said*,
>> "Let the waters under the heaven be gathered…"
>
> And God *said*,
>> "Let the earth bring forth grass…"
>
> And God *said*,
>> "Let the waters bring forth abundantly the moving creature that hath life…"
>
> And God *said*,
>> "Let us make man in our image, after our likeness: and let them have dominion over the fish of the sea, and over the fowl of the air, and over the

> cattle, and over all the earth, and over every creep-
> ing thing the creepeth upon the earth."
>
> Genesis 1:3–28 (KJV)

Right there in the book of Genesis it tells us that with words God spoke and created everything. God said, and it became visible. And he is telling us that we have authority over everything when we speak in the name of Jesus. And that means authority over the enemy as well. God spoke the words to create the world and everything in it. But us he did create and form from the dust of the ground. And he breathed into the nostrils the breath of life, and man became a living soul. Therefore, we are made of the dust of the ground, and God plants his seed of word in us, in our hearts, and as we water them by reading them and applying them to our lives, they are able to grow. God's words are incorruptible seeds. When we read his Word or hear his Word, they become seeds planted within us. Every time we speak them, believe in them, rely on them, and *apply* them in our daily lives, it is like watering them, and then we can produce a harvest from speaking his Word.

Likewise, look at the ships; though they are so great and are driven by rough winds, they are steered by a very small rudder wherever the impulse of the helmsman determines. Even so the tongue is a little member, and it can boast of great things. See how much wood or how great a forest a tiny spark can set ablaze.

James 3:4–5

What God is saying here is that you can determine the direction and outcome of every situation that you find yourself in. You must think about this and pray about this ahead of time, before you go to sleep at night and before you get up in the morning. Ask God for his guidance and wisdom so that you are aware of the fact that your words can bless or curse. We need to very seriously consider how we speak and of all the damaging words that we consider insignificant and then pass off by saying, "Oh. I did not mean it." But you spoke it, and the spoken word is either a blessing or a curse. And as we remember back in Galatians 5:22 (NLT), "But when the Holy Spirit controls our lives he will produce this kind of fruit in us; love, joy, peace, patience ... and self control ..." Think on and realize that your words and what you speak can actually determine the outcome of every situation. You must realize that thoughts come before words. So learn to become conscious of what you are thinking, and let the Holy Spirit lead you so that you will not curse but bless. Now you know that you are renewing your mind. Therefore, you are renewing your thinking. Change begins with words. Therefore, your thoughts (way of thinking with knowledgeable information) are responsible for how you make a decision. Your decision results in your actions, and your actions will become your habits. Your habits create your character, which directs your destination. "You therefore, must be perfect [growing into complete maturity of godliness in mind and character..." (Matthew 5:48).

You also need to understand that the enemy also knows the importance of our words, and he will be trying very hard to convince you that you have no authority in your words—especially if you do not see any immediate results. But our faith and patience will bring God's words to manifest.

> Out of the same mouth come forth blessing and cursing. These things, my brethren, ought not to be so. Does a fountain send forth [si-

multaneously] from the same opening fresh
water and bitter?

James 3:10–11

That scripture is saying to us that what comes out of
our mouths (our words) can bless someone or they
can curse someone. You must determine what kind of
character (spirit, moral fiber) you are going to choose
to be. And God is telling us that we should not use
our mouths and our words for both blessing and curs-
ing. We should always choose to bless. Speaking well
of someone is blessing them.

Let no foul *or* polluting language, *nor* evil
word *nor* unwholesome *or* worthless talk
[ever] come out of your mouth, but only such
[speech] as is good *and* beneficial to the spiritual progress of others, as is fitting to the need
and the occasion, that it may be a blessing *and*
give grace (God's favor) to those who hear it.

Ephesians 4:29

When your loved one hears you speak well of them,
they receive God's grace. They receive worthiness,
respect, security, and love. What is in our hearts, not

our misguided emotions, is what should come forth out of our mouths. And by now, we should have in our hearts forgiveness, compassion, and love. I know that it is hard to hold back and control your tongue when you are angry or when you feel disappointed, but you know in truth that you yourself can hold back and control what you say. Just think of a time when you had to refrain from saying something that you may have liked to say, but the person was either a boss that you had to control your feelings in front of, or a friend that you did not want to offend, or someone you respected and did not want them to think less of you. At that time, you were able to control how you spoke. And now you have the Holy Spirit to help as well. So, you see, you *can* control how you choose to speak. This may not be a real easy step for you, but with the Holy Spirit guiding you, you should get better and better at it.

> A soft answer turns away wrath, but Grievous words stir up anger.
>
> Proverbs 15:1 (KJV)

Think about how you have spoken in the past. I'm sure I can recreate a scene that you can relate to.

Think about when you have heard it in their voice, or you have seen it in their eyes or watched their actions telling you they are under the influence of alcohol or some other substance, and immediately, you took a breath, closed your eyes, and felt that sinking emotion coming up within you and, without thinking (without your new mindset), you have said something like, "I can't believe you are in this condition again. I thought that at least today you would show some sort of unselfishness, but no, all you care about is yourself and getting drunk or high. You are such a loser. I can't stand you. You are never going to change. What am I going to tell everybody? You are just like your father. You are going to kill yourself and me. Why are you doing this?" Does that scene sound familiar? And has speaking to them with those words produced any healing? My guess would be no. But now, with your new knowledge and new thinking, try, when you are faced with this situation, to take that breath and think, *I know why they are in that condition. They are afflicted, and my rash words will only make it worse. I will not curse them further. I will comfort them and speak words that will heal and not curse.*

Anxiety in a man's heart weights it down, but
an encouraging word makes it glad.

Proverbs 12:25

It is an honor for a man to cease from strife *and*
keep aloof from it, but every fool will quarrel.

Proverbs 19:11

Remember, to the afflicted, their days are filled with
anxious (worried, concerned, uneasy, frightened, rest-
less, and nervous, guilt-filled) thoughts. I am sure that
in your particular situation, you could say something
of an encouraging nature. With the love in your heart,
you could say something like, "Next time, I am sure
you will be able to join us," or, "I know that someday
soon we will be able to go back to that cabin in the
woods and have a great time. I am looking forward
to it, and I hope you are too." Put some hope of the
future in their lives. Let them know that you are positive and looking forward to a future with them. Never,
never bring up a past offense. And if they do, just tell
them, "That is in the past," and that you have forgotten it and that they too should forget it. Remember,
you have let it go. And you are speaking words with
your new, forgiving nature.

Try to pay attention to even the smallest positive action or words that your loved one might do or speak. Then acknowledge it in a normal, positive way. Even in the slightest of effort on their part to contribute a hand to you, thank them, not making it a big issue, just in a meek, normal, natural way. Or if they say something positive, just say something like, "That's good thinking," and add a little smile of approval with it.

> Pleasant words are as a honeycomb, sweet to
> the mind and healing to the body.
> Proverbs 16:24

They need their self-worth built up. No matter what you see, their inner thinking of their self-worth is pretty low. Your kind words are sweet to the mind (can replace all those anxious thoughts) and heal them. Remember that your adversary is going to try to prevent you from speaking kindly. We listened to him long enough. Now we are doing it God's way. Your words are *powerful*—not just your kind words; your harsh words are just as effective, but in a destructive way. I am sure that when you soften your response to a situation such as mentioned above, it will not put the afflicted person (your loved one) on the defense, and you will have harvested some peace in your life already.

> A gentle tongue [with its healing power] is a tree of life, but willful contrariness in it breaks down the spirit.
>
> Proverbs 15:4

You need to lift their spirit, not break their spirit. When you learn the correct words and how to apply them, you will find that you will be able to open up a line of communication with your loved ones. They will begin to trust that you are not going to fly off the handle and just start condemning them. But you are showing them that you will remain calm and steady and be understanding and that they really do matter. They will begin to open up to you. They need someone they can trust and rely on.

When things seem to be hopeless, speak of God's hope. When things seem to be discouraging, speak of God's encouragement. Start guarding your heart (the ground where word seeds are planted). Do not let unkind words in to take root. If someone starts to speak unkindly of your loved ones, stop them.

Let them know that their words as well can hold the power of death or life, a blessing or a curse, and ask them to speak healing words instead.

> For often your own heart knows that you have likewise cursed others.
>
> Ecclesiastes 7:22

> Set a guard, O Lord, before my mouth; keep watch at the door of my lips.
>
> Psalm 141:3

We have all spoken things that we are truly sorry for saying. This is where we ask and receive forgiveness (let it go) and pray that the Lord help us to keep watch over our mouths. Set your mind to speak only blessings over your loved one.

> Bless the Lord, ye his angels, that excel in strength, that do his commandments, harkening unto the voice of his word.
>
> Psalm 103:19

You are the voice of his words. Speak his words out loud. Shout them with confidence of your authority in Jesus. You are in a battle, and God says to fight the good fight of faith.

> Then said the Lord to me, You have seen well, for I am alert *and* active, watching over My word to perform it.
>
> Jeremiah 1:12

When They Say That There Is Nothing You Can Do

You will now be able to say, "There is so very much I can do, and I will no longer be deceived of the truth."

- I can do all things through Christ who strengthens me.
- I am building a strong foundation toward recovery for my loved one and our family. I

know it is a process, and I know that recovery is possible.

- My loved one and I have the faith we need.

- I have *set my mind*, and I am keeping it set.

- I am learning to love and live by faith, not by my feelings.

- I have put my hope in God.

- I believe in God's promises.

- God has heard my prayers, and I have humbled myself before him.

- I am renewing my mind *daily* with God's words, resulting in a fresh and new attitude.

- I am not alone in this affliction.

- *Daily*, I pray for others to achieve their healing. I know our prayers are powerful.

- I know that this is a spiritual war and that I have the right warfare (love, forgiveness and speaking God's words) to win it with.

- I understand the benefits, abilities, and power of forgiveness.

- I have the knowledge of the power and ability of my words and God's strength behind them.

- I am aware now of the enemy's ways and how he will try to take the Word from me if I do not sow it in my heart. Because if I do not have it in my heart and know them, I will not have the knowledge I need.

- I understand that the enemy lies to my loved one, causing anxiety.

There are many ways to hear God's words today. There is the Bible (the best source, of course) and there are concordance books to help you look up certain scriptures that contain subjects you need. You can look up any word, and it will give you the reference of all the scriptures containing that word. If you look up *love*, you will find many, many scriptures that tell you about that subject.

There are many programs on television, at any given time of day, that teach God's Word and his way. And as you watch them, take notes so that you can look the information up in the Bible and read it for yourself. The reason I say you need to read the Bible yourself is so that you are not misled by anyone trying to twist God's words.

Just one example: You know the saying, "Cleanliness

is next to godliness." Well, that was taken out of context from the book of 1 Peter 3:21. The Bible is referring to an inward cleanness of your spirit. But that is just a sample of how people can twist God's Word and their meaning. There is the Internet, with some very good commentary of the Bible, which goes into detail and can give you a better understanding. This is something you need to apply to your life every day. At least give your attention of some measure to God's Word every day so that you can be encouraged. And know that every day someone is praying for you and your family and believing that you and your loved one will overcome this affliction. May God bless you and your family.

> Practice what you have learned and received and heard and seen in me, and model your way of living on it, and the God of peace (of untroubled, undisturbed well-being) will be with you.
>
> Philippians 4:9